DAUBER

DAUBER

A POEM

BY

JOHN MASEFIELD

AUTHOR OF
"THE EVERLASTING MERCY," ETC.

LONDON
WILLIAM HEINEMANN
MCMXIII

Copyright

TO

MY WIFE

NOTE

I thank the editor and proprietors of the *English Review* for permitting me to reprint this poem, which first appeared in their issue for October, 1912.

DAUBER

I

Four bells were struck, the watch was called on deck,
All work aboard was over for the hour,
And some men sang and others played at check,
Or mended clothes or watched the sunset glower.
The bursting west was like an opening flower,
And one man watched it till the light was dim,
But no one went across to talk to him.

He was the painter in that swift ship's crew—
Lampman and painter—tall, a slight-built man,
Young for his years, and not yet twenty-two;
Sickly, and not yet brown with the sea's tan.
Bullied and damned at since the voyage began,
"Being neither man nor seaman by his tally,"
He bunked with the idlers just abaft the galley.

DAUBER

His work began at five ; he worked all day,
Keeping no watch and having all night in.
His work was what the mate might care to say ;
He mixed red lead in many a bouilli tin ;
His dungarees were smeared with paraffin.
" Go drown himself " his round-house mates advised
    him,
And all hands called him " Dauber " and despised him.

Si, the apprentice, stood beside the spar,
Stripped to the waist, a basin at his side,
Slushing his hands to get away the tar,
And then he washed himself and rinsed and dried ;
Towelling his face, hair-towzelled, eager-eyed,
He crossed the spar to Dauber, and there stood
Watching the gold of heaven turn to blood.

They stood there by the rail while the swift ship
Tore on out of the tropics, straining her sheets,
Whitening her trackway to a milky strip,
Dim with green bubbles and twisted water-meets,
Her clacking tackle tugged at pins and cleats,
Her great sails bellied stiff, her great masts leaned :
They watched how the seas struck and burst and
    greened.

2

DAUBER

Si talked with Dauber, standing by the side.
" Why did you come to sea, painter ?" he said.
" I want to be a painter," he replied,
" And know the sea and ships from A to Z,
And paint great ships at sea before I'm dead ;
Ships under skysails running down the Trade—
Ships and the sea ; there's nothing finer made.

" But there's so much to learn, with sails and ropes,
And how the sails look, full or being furled,
And how the lights change in the troughs and slopes,
And the sea's colours up and down the world,
And how a storm looks when the sprays are hurled
High as the yard (they say) I want to see ;
There's none ashore can teach such things to me.

" And then the men and rigging, and the way
Ships move, running or beating, and the poise
At the roll's end, the checking in the sway—
I want to paint them perfect, short of the noise ;
And then the life, the half-decks full of boys,
The fo'c'sles with the men there, dripping wet :
I know the subjects that I want to get.

3

DAUBER

" It's not been done, the sea, not yet been done,
From the inside, by one who really knows ;
I'd give up all if I could be the one,
But art comes dear the way the money goes.
So I have come to sea, and I suppose
Three years will teach me all I want to learn
And make enough to keep me till I earn."

Even as he spoke his busy pencil moved,
Drawing the leap of water off the side
Where the great clipper trampled iron-hooved,
Making the blue hills of the sea divide,
Shearing a glittering scatter in her stride,
And leaping on full tilt with all sails drawing,
Proud as a war-horse, snuffing battle, pawing.

" I cannot get it yet—not yet," he said ;
" That leap and light, and sudden change to green,
And all the glittering from the sunset's red,
And the milky colours where the bursts have been,
And then the clipper striding like a queen
Over it all, all beauty to the crown.
I see it all, I cannot put it down.

4

DAUBER

" It's hard not to be able.   There, look there !
I cannot get the movement nor the light ;
Sometimes it almost makes a man despair
To try and try and never get it right.
Oh, if I could—oh, if I only might,
I wouldn't mind what hells I'd have to pass,
Not if the whole world called me fool and ass."

Down sank the crimson sun into the sea,
The wind cut chill at once, the west grew dun.
" Out sidelights !" called the mate. " Hi, where is he ?"
The Boatswain called, " Out sidelights, damn you !
        Run !"
" He's always late or lazing," murmured one—
" The Dauber, with his sketching."   Soon the tints
Of red and green passed on dark water-glints.

Darker it grew, still darker, and the stars
Burned golden, and the fiery fishes came.
The wire-note loudened from the straining spars ;
The sheet-blocks clacked together always the same ;
The rushing fishes streaked the seas with flame,
Racing the one speed noble as their own :
What unknown joy was in those fish unknown !

DAUBER

Just by the round-house door, as it grew dark,
The Boatswain caught the Dauber with, " Now, you ;
Till now I've spared you, damn you ! now you hark :
I've just had hell for what you didn't do ;
I'll have you broke and sent among the crew
If you get me more trouble by a particle.
Don't you forget, you daubing, useless article !

"You thing, you twice-laid thing from Port Mahon !"
Then came the Cook's " Is that the Dauber there ?
Why don't you leave them stinking paints alone ?
They stink the house out, poisoning all the air.
Just take them out."   "Where to ?"   " I don't care
     where.
I won't have stinking paint here."   From their plates :
"That's right; wet paint breeds fever," growled his
     mates.

He took his still wet drawings from the berth
And climbed the ladder to the deck-house top ;
Beneath, the noisy half-deck rang with mirth,
For two ship's boys were putting on the strop :
One, clambering up to let the skylight drop,
Saw him bend down beneath a boat and lay
His drawings there, till all were hid away,

6

And stand there silent, leaning on the boat,
Watching the constellations rise and burn,
Until the beauty took him by the throat,
So stately is their glittering overturn;
Armies of marching eyes, armies that yearn
With banners rising and falling, and passing by
Over the empty silence of the sky.

The Dauber sighed there looking at the sails,
Wind-steadied arches leaning on the night,
The high trucks traced on heaven and left no trails;
The moonlight made the topsails almost white,
The passing sidelight seemed to drip green light.
And on the clipper rushed with fire-bright bows;
He sighed, " I'll never do 't," and left the house.

" Now," said the reefer, "up ! Come, Sam ; come, Si,
Dauber's been hiding something." Up they slid,
Treading on naked tiptoe stealthily
To grope for treasure at the long boat skid.
" Drawings !" said Sam. "Is this what Dauber hid ?
Lord ! I expected pudding, not this rot.
Still, come, we'll have some fun with what we've got."

DAUBER

They smeared the paint with turpentine until
They could remove with mess-clouts every trace
Of quick perception caught by patient skill,
And lines that had brought blood into his face.
They wiped the pigments off, and did erase,
With knives, all sticking clots.   When they had done,
Under the boat they laid them every one.

All he had drawn since first he came to sea,
His six weeks' leisure's fruits, they laid them there.
They chuckled then to think how mad he'd be
Finding his paintings vanished into air.
Eight bells were struck, and feet from everywhere
Went shuffling aft to muster in the dark ;
The mate's pipe glowed above, a dim red spark.

Names in the darkness passed and voices cried ;
The red spark glowed and died, the faces seemed
As things remembered when a brain has died,
To all but high intenseness deeply dreamed.
Like hissing spears the fishes' fire streamed,
And on the clipper rushed with tossing mast,
A bath of flame broke round her as she passed.

DAUBER

The watch was set, the night came, and the men
Hid from the moon in shadowed nooks to sleep,
Bunched like the dead; still, like the dead, as when
Plague in a city leaves none even to weep.
The ship's track brightened to a mile-broad sweep;
The mate there felt her pulse, and eyed the spars:
South-west by south she staggered under the stars.

Down in his bunk the Dauber lay awake
Thinking of his unfitness for the sea.
Each failure, each derision, each mistake,
There in the life not made for such as he;
A morning grim with trouble sure to be,
A noon of pain from failure, and a night
Bitter with men's contemning and despite.

This in the first beginning, the green leaf,
Still in the Trades before bad weather fell;
What harvest would he reap of hate and grief
When the loud Horn made every life a hell?
When the sick ship lay over, clanging her bell,
And no time came for painting or for drawing,
But all hands fought, and icy death came clawing?

9

DAUBER

Hell, he expected,—hell. His eyes grew blind ;
The snoring from his messmates droned and snuffled,
And then a gush of pity calmed his mind.
The cruel torment of his thought was muffled,
Without, on deck, an old, old seaman shuffled,
Humming his song, and through the open door
A moonbeam moved and thrust along the floor.

The green bunk curtains moved, the brass rings
    clicked,
The Cook cursed in his sleep, turning and turning,
The moonbeam's moving finger touched and picked,
And all the stars in all the sky were burning.
"This is the art I've come for, and am learning,
The sea and ships and men and travelling things.
It is most proud, whatever pain it brings."

He leaned upon his arm and watched the light
Sliding and fading to the steady roll ;
This he would some day paint, the ship at night,
And sleeping seamen tired to the soul ;
The space below the bunks as black as coal,
Gleams upon chests, upon the unlit lamp,
The ranging door-hook, and the locker clamp.

10

DAUBER

This he would paint, and that, and all these scenes,
And proud ships carrying on, and men their minds,
And blues of rollers toppling into greens,
And shattering into white that bursts and blinds,
And scattering ships running erect like hinds,
And men in oilskins beating down a sail
High on the yellow yard, in snow, in hail,

With faces ducked down from the slanting drive
Of half-thawed hail mixed with half-frozen spray,
The roaring canvas, like a thing alive,
Shaking the mast, knocking their hands away,
The foot-ropes jerking to the tug and sway,
The savage eyes salt-reddened at the rims,
And icicles on the south-wester brims.

And sunnier scenes would grow under his brush,
The tropic dawn with all things dropping dew,
The darkness and the wonder and the hush,
The insensate grey before the marvel grew ;
Then the veil lifted from the trembling blue,
The walls of sky burst in, the flower, the rose,
All the expanse of heaven a mind that glows.

DAUBER

He turned out of his bunk ; the Cook still tossed,
One of the other two spoke in his sleep,
A cockroach scuttled where the moonbeam crossed ;
Outside there was the ship, the night, the deep.
" It is worth while," the youth said ; " I will keep
To my resolve, I'll learn to paint all this.
My Lord, my God, how beautiful it is !"

Outside was the ship's rush to the wind's hurry,
A resonant wire-hum from every rope,
The broadening bow-wash in a fiery flurry,
The leaning masts in their majestic slope,
And all things strange with moonlight : filled with
    hope
By all that beauty going as man bade,
He turned and slept in peace.   Eight bells were
    made.

II

Next day was Sunday, his free painting day,
While the fine weather held, from eight till eight.
He rose when called at five, and did array
The round-house gear, and set the kit-bags straight;
Then kneeling down, like housemaid at a grate,
He scrubbed the deck with sand until his knees
Were blue with dye from his wet dungarees.

Soon all was clean, his Sunday tasks were done;
His day was clear for painting as he chose.
The wetted decks were drying in the sun,
The men coiled up, or swabbed, or sought repose.
The drifts of silver arrows fell and rose
As flying fish took wing; the breakfast passed,
Wasting good time, but he was free at last.

DAUBER

Free for two hours and more to tingle deep,
Catching a likeness in a line or tint,
The canvas running up in a proud sweep,
Wind-wrinkled at the clews, and white like lint,
The glittering of the blue waves into glint ;
Free to attempt it all, the proud ship's pawings,
The sea, the sky—he went to fetch his drawings.

Up to the deck-house top he quickly climbed,
He stooped to find them underneath the boat.
He found them all obliterated, slimed,
Blotted, erased, gone from him line and note.
They were all spoiled : a lump came in his throat,
Being vain of his attempts, and tender skinned—
Beneath the skylight watching reefers grinned.

He clambered down, holding the ruined things.
"Bosun," he called, "look here, did you do these :
Wipe off my paints and cut them into strings,
And smear them till you can't tell chalk from cheese ?
Don't stare, but did you do it ?   Answer, please."
The Bosun turned : " I'll give you a thick ear !
Do it ?   I didn't.   Get to hell from here !

DAUBER

"I touch your stinking daubs?   The Dauber's daft."
A crowd was gathering now to hear the fun ;
The reefers tumbled out, the men laid aft,
The Cook blinked, cleaning a mess-kid in the sun.
"What's up with Dauber now?" said everyone.
"Someone has spoiled my drawings—look at this !"
"Well, that's a dirty trick, by God, it is !"

"It is," said Sam, "a low-down dirty trick,
To spoil a fellow's work in such a way,
And if you catch him, Dauber, punch him sick,
For he deserves it, be he who he may."
A seaman shook his old head wise and grey.
"It seems to me," he said, "who ain't no judge,
Them drawings look much better now they're smudge."

"Where were they, Dauber?   On the deck-house ?
        Where ?"
"Under the long-boat, in a secret place."
"The blackguard must have seen you put them there.
He is a swine !   I tell him to his face :
I didn't think we'd anyone so base."
"Nor I," said Dauber.   "There was six weeks' time
Just wasted in these drawings: it's a crime !"

DAUBER

" Well, don't you say we did it," growled his mates
" And as for crime, be damned ! the things were
     smears—
Best overboard, like you, with shot for weights ;
Thank God they're gone, and now go shake your ears."
The Dauber listened, very near to tears.
" Dauber, if I were you," said Sam again,
" I'd aft, and see the Captain and complain."

A sigh came from the assembled seamen there.
Would he be such a fool for their delight
As go to tell the Captain ?   Would he dare ?
And would the thunder roar, the lightning smite ?
There was the Captain come to take a sight,
Handling his sextant by the chart-house aft.
The Dauber turned, the seamen thought him daft.

The Captain took his sights—a mate below
Noted the times ; they shouted to each other,
The Captain quick with " Stop," the answer slow,
Repeating slowly one height then another.
The swooping clipper stumbled through the smother,
The ladder brasses in the sunlight burned,
The Dauber waited till the Captain turned.

16

DAUBER

There stood the Dauber, humbled to the bone,
Waiting to speak. The Captain let him wait,
Glanced at the course, and called in even tone,
"What is the man there wanting, Mr. Mate?"
The logship clattered on the grating straight,
The reel rolled to the scuppers with a clatter,
The Mate came grim: "Well, Dauber, what's the
    matter?"

"Please, sir, they spoiled my drawings." "Who
    did?" "They."
"Who's they?" "I don't quite know, sir."
"Don't quite know, sir?
Then why are you aft to talk about it,
    hey?
Whom d'you complain of?" "No one." "No one?"
    "No, sir."
"Well, then, go forward till you've found them. Go,
    sir.
If you complain of someone, then I'll see.
Now get to hell! and don't come bothering
    me."

DAUBER

"But, sir, they washed them off, and some they cut.
Look here, sir, how they spoiled them." "Never mind.
Go shove your head inside the scuttle butt,
And that will make you cooler.   You will find
Nothing like water when you're mad and blind.
Where were the drawings ? in your chest, or where ?"
"Under the long-boat, sir ; I put them there."

"Under the long-boat, hey ?   Now mind your tip.
I'll have the skids kept clear with nothing round them ;
The long-boat ain't a store in this here ship.
Lucky for you it wasn't I who found them.
If I had seen them, Dauber, I'd have drowned them.
Now you be warned by this.   I tell you plain—
Don't stow your brass-rags under boats again.

"Go forward to your berth."   The Dauber turned.
The listeners down below them winked and smiled,
Knowing how red the Dauber's temples burned,
Having lost the case about his only child.
His work was done to nothing and defiled,
And there was no redress : the Captain's voice
Spoke, and called "Painter," making him rejoice.

DAUBER

The Captain and the Mate conversed together.
"Drawings, you tell me, Mister?" "Yes, sir; views:
Wiped off with turps, I gather that's his blether.
He says they're things he can't afford to lose.
He's Dick, who came to sea in dancing shoes,
And found the dance a bear dance. They were hidden
Under the long-boat's chocks, which I've forbidden."

"Wiped off with turps?" The Captain sucked his lip.
"Who did it, Mister?" "Reefers, I suppose;
Them devils do the most pranks in a ship;
The round-house might have done it, Cook or Bose.'
"I can't take notice of it till he knows.
How does he do his work?" "Well, no offence;
He tries; he does his best. He's got no sense."

"Painter," the Captain called; the Dauber came.
"What's all this talk of drawings? What's the matter?"
"They spoiled my drawings, sir." "Well, who's to
      blame?
The long-boat's there for no one to get at her;
You broke the rules, and if you choose to scatter
Gear up and down where it's no right to be,
And suffer as result, don't come to me.

DAUBER

" Your place is in the round-house, and your gear
Belongs where you belong. Who spoiled your things?
Find out who spoiled your things and fetch him here."
" But, sir, they cut the canvas into strings."
" I want no argument nor questionings.
Go back where you belong and say no more,
And please remember that you're not on shore."

The Dauber touched his brow and slunk away—
They eyed his going with a bitter eye.
" Dauber," said Sam, " what did the Captain say?"
The Dauber drooped his head without reply.
" Go forward, Dauber, and enjoy your cry."
The Mate limped to the rail; like little feet
Over his head the drumming reef-points beat.

The Dauber reached the berth and entered in.
Much mockery followed after as he went,
And each face seemed to greet him with the grin
Of hounds hot following on a creature spent.
" Aren't you a fool?" each mocking visage meant.
" Who did it, Dauber?   What did Captain say?
It is a crime, and there'll be hell to pay."

DAUBER

He bowed his head, the house was full of smoke ;
The Sails was pointing shackles on his chest.
" Lord, Dauber, be a man and take a joke "—
He puffed his pipe—" and let the matter rest.
Spit brown, my son, and get a hairy breast ;
Get shoulders on you at the crojick braces,
And let this painting business go to blazes.

" What good can painting do to anyone ?
I don't say never do it ; far from that—
No harm in sometimes painting just for fun.
Keep it for fun, and stick to what you're at.
Your job's to fill your bones up and get fat ;
Rib up like Barney's bull, and thick your neck.
Throw paints to hell, boy ; you belong on deck."

" That's right," said Chips ; " it's downright good
    advice.
Painting's no good ; what good can painting do
Up on a lower topsail stiff with ice,
With all your little fish-hooks frozen blue ?
Painting won't help you at the weather clew,
Nor pass your gaskets for you, nor make sail.
Painting's a balmy job not worth a nail."

DAUBER

The Dauber did not answer; time was passing.
He pulled his easel out, his paints, his stool.
The wind was dropping, and the sea was glassing—
New realms of beauty waited for his rule;
The draught out of the crojick kept him cool.
He sat to paint, alone and melancholy.
"No turning fools," the Chips said, "from their
    folly."

He dipped his brush and tried to fix a line,
And then came peace, and gentle beauty came,
Turning his spirit's water into wine,
Lightening his darkness with a touch of flame:
O, joy of trying for beauty, ever the same,
You never fail, your comforts never end;
O, balm of this world's way; O, perfect friend!

III

THEY lost the Trades soon after ; then came calm,
Light little gusts and rain, which soon increased
To glorious northers shouting out a psalm
At seeing the bright blue water silver fleeced ;
Hornwards she rushed, trampling the seas to yeast.
There fell a rain-squall in a blind day's end
When for an hour the Dauber found a friend.

Out of the rain the voices called and passed,
The staysails flogged, the tackle yanked and shook.
Inside the harness-room a lantern cast
Light and wild shadows as it ranged its hook.
The watch on deck was gathered in the nook,
They had taken shelter in that secret place,
Wild light gave wild emotions to each face.

23

DAUBER

One beat the beef-cask, and the others sang
A song that had brought anchors out of seas
In ports where bells of Christians never rang,
Nor any sea mark blazed among the trees.
By forlorn swamps, in ice, by windy keys,
That song had sounded ; now it shook the air
From these eight wanderers brought together there.

Under the poop-break, sheltering from the rain,
The Dauber sketched some likeness of the room,
A note to be a prompting to his brain,
A spark to make old memory reillume.
" Dauber," said someone near him in the gloom,
" How goes it, Dauber ?"   It was reefer Si.
" There's not much use in trying to keep dry."

They sat upon the sail-room doorway coaming,
The lad held forth like youth, the Dauber listened
To how the boy had had a taste for roaming,
And what the sea is said to be and isn't.
Where the dim lamplight fell the wet deck glistened.
Si said the Horn was still some weeks away,
" But tell me, Dauber, where d'you hail from ?   Eh ?"

DAUBER

The rain blew past and let the stars appear ;
The seas grew larger as the moonlight grew
For half an hour the ring of heaven was clear,
Dusty with moonlight, grey rather than blue ;
In that great moon the showing stars were few.
The sleepy time-boy's feet passed overhead.
"I come from out past Gloucester," Dauber said ;

" Not far from Pauntley, if you know those parts ;
The place is Spital Farm, near Silver Hill,
Above a trap-hatch where a mill-stream starts.
We had the mill once, but we've stopped the mill ;
My dad and sister keep the farm on still.
We're only tenants, but we've rented there,
Father and son, for over eighty year.

" Father has worked the farm since grandfer went ;
It means the world to him ; I can't think why
They bleed him to the last half-crown for rent,
And this and that have almost milked him dry.
The land's all starved ; if he'd put money by,
And corn was up, and rent was down two-thirds. . .
But then they aren't, so what's the use of words.

DAUBER

" Yet still he couldn't bear to see it pass
To strangers, or to think a time would come
When other men than us would mow the grass,
And other names than ours have the home.
Some sorrows come from evil thought, but some
Comes when two men are near, and both are blind
To what is generous in the other's mind.

" I was the only boy, and father thought
I'd farm the Spital after he was dead,
And many a time he took me out and taught
About manures and seed-corn white and red,
And soils and hops, but I'd an empty head ;
Harvest or seed, I would not do a turn—
I loathed the farm, I didn't want to learn.

' He did not mind at first, he thought it youth
Feeling the collar, and that I should change.
Then time gave him some inklings of the truth,
And that I loathed the farm, and wished to range.
Truth to a man of fifty's always strange ;
It was most strange and terrible to him
That I, his heir, should be the devil's limb.

26

DAUBER

" Yet still he hoped the Lord might change my mind.
I'd see him bridle in his wrath and hate,
And almost break my heart he was so kind,
Biting his lips sore with resolve to wait.
And then I'd try awhile ; but it was Fate :
I didn't want to learn ; the farm to me
Was mire and hopeless work and misery.

" Though there were things I loved about it, too —
The beasts, the apple-trees, and going haying.
And then I tried ; but no, it wouldn't do,
The farm was prison, and my thoughts were straying.
And there'd come father, with his grey head, praying,
' O, my dear son, don't let the Spital pass ;
It's my old home, boy, where your grandfer was.

" ' And now you won't learn farming ; you don't care.
The old home's nought to you.   I've tried to teach you ;
I've begged Almighty God, boy, all I dare,
To use His hand if word of mine won't reach you.
Boy, for your granfer's sake I do beseech you,
Don't let the Spital pass to strangers.   Squire
Has said he'd give it you if we require.

DAUBER

" ' Your mother used to walk here, boy, with me
It was her favourite walk down to the mill;
And there we'd talk how little death would be,
Knowing our work was going on here still.
You've got the brains, you only want the will—
Don't disappoint your mother and your father.
I'll give you time to travel, if you'd rather.'

" But, no, I'd wander up the brooks to read.
Then sister Jane would start with nagging tongue,
Saying my sin made father's heart to bleed,
And how she feared she'd live to see me hung.
And then she'd read me bits from Dr. Young.
And when we three would sit to supper, Jane
Would fillip dad till dad began again.

" ' I've been here all my life, boy.   I was born
Up in the room above—looks on the mead.
I never thought you'd cockle my clean corn,
And leave the old home to a stranger's seed.
Father and I have made here 'thout a weed:
We've give our lives to make that.   Eighty years.
And now I go down to the grave in tears.'

DAUBER

" And then I'd get ashamed and take off coat,
And work maybe a week, ploughing and sowing
And then I'd creep away and sail my boat,
Or watch the water when the mill was going.
That's my delight—to be near water flowing,
Dabbling or sailing boats or jumping stanks,
Or finding moorhens' nests along the banks.

" And one day father found a ship I'd built ;
He took the cart-whip to me over that,
And I, half mad with pain, and sick with guilt,
Went up and hid in what we called the flat,
A dusty hole given over to the cat.
She kittened there ; the kittens had worn paths
Among the cobwebs, dust, and broken laths.

" And putting down my hand between the beams
I felt a leathery thing, and pulled it clear :
A book with white cocoons stuck in the seams,
Where spiders had had nests for many a year.
It was my mother's sketch-book ; hid, I fear,
Lest dad should ever see it.   Mother's life
Was not her own while she was father's wife.

29

DAUBER

" There were her drawings, dated, pencilled faint.
March was the last one, eighteen eighty-three,
Unfinished that, for tears had smeared the paint.
The rest was landscape, not yet brought to be.
That was a holy afternoon to me ;
That book a sacred book ; the flat a place
Where I could meet my mother face to face.

" She had found peace of spirit, mother had,
Drawing the landscape from the attic there—
Heart-broken, often, after rows with dad,
Hid like a wild thing in a secret lair.
That rotting sketch-book showed me how and where
I, too, could get away ; and then I knew
That drawing was the work I longed to do.

" Drawing became my life.   I drew, I toiled,
And every penny I could get I spent
On paints and artist's matters, which I spoiled
Up in the attic to my heart's content,
Till one day father asked me what I meant ;
The time had come, he said, to make an end.
Now it must finish : what did I intend ?

30

DAUBER

" Either I took to farming, like his son,
In which case he would teach me, early and late
(Provided that my daubing mood was done),
Or I must go : it must be settled straight.
If I refused to farm, there was the gate.
I was to choose, his patience was all gone,
The present state of things could not go on.

" Sister was there ; she eyed me while he spoke.
The kitchen clock ran down and struck the hour,
And something told me father's heart was broke,
For all he stood so set and looked so sour.
Jane took a duster, and began to scour
A pewter on the dresser ; she was crying.
I stood stock still a long time, not replying.

" Dad waited, then he snorted and turned round.
' Well, think of it,' he said.   He left the room,
His boots went clop along the stony ground
Out to the orchard and the apple-bloom.
A cloud came past the sun and made a gloom ;
I swallowed with dry lips, then sister turned.
She was dead white but for her eyes that burned.

31

DAUBER

"'You're breaking father's heart, Joe," she began;
'It's not as if——' she checked, in too much pain.
'O, Joe, don't help to kill so fine a man;
You're giving him our mother over again.
It's wearing him to death, Joe, heart and brain;
You know what store he sets on leaving this
To (it's too cruel) to a son of his.

"'Yet you go painting all the day.   O, Joe,
Couldn't you make an effort?   Can't you see
What folly it is of yours?   It's not as though
You are a genius, or could ever be.
O, Joe, for father's sake, if not for me,
Give up this craze for painting, and be wise
And work with father, where your duty lies.'

"'It goes too deep,' I said; 'I loathe the farm;
I couldn't help, even if I'd the mind.
Even if I helped, I'd only do him harm;
Father would see it, if he were not blind.
I was not built to farm, as he would find.
O, Jane, it's bitter hard to stand alone
And spoil my father's life or spoil my own.'

32

DAUBER

" ' Spoil both,' she said, ' the way you're shaping now.
You're only a boy not knowing your own good.
Where will you go, suppose you leave here? How
Do you propose to earn your daily food?
Draw? Daub the pavements? There's a feckless
    brood
Goes to the devil daily, Joe, in cities
Only from thinking how divine their wit is.

" ' Clouds are they, without water, carried away.
And you'll be one of them, the way you're going,
Daubing at silly pictures all the day,
And praised by silly fools who're always blowing.
And you choose this when you might go a-sowing,
Casting the good corn into chosen mould
That shall in time bring forth a hundredfold.'

" So we went on, but in the end it ended.
I felt I'd done a murder; I felt sick.
There's much in human minds cannot be mended,
And that, not I, played dad a cruel trick.
There was one mercy: that it ended quick.
I went to join my mother's brother: he
Lived down the Severn. He was kind to me.

DAUBER

" And there I learned house-painting for a living.
I'd have been happy there, but that I knew
I'd sinned before my father past forgiving,
And that they sat at home, that silent two,
Wearing the fire out and the evening through,
Silent, defeated, broken, in despair,
My plate unset, my name gone, and my chair.

" I saw all that; and sister Jane came white—
White as a ghost, with fiery, weeping eyes.
I saw her all day long and half the night,
Bitter as gall, and passionate and wise.
' Joe, you have killed your father: there he lies.
You have done your work—you with our mother's
     ways.'
She said it plain, and then her eyes would blaze.

" And then one day I had a job to do
Down below bridge, by where the docks begin,
And there I saw a clipper towing through,
Up from the sea that morning, entering in.
Raked to the nines she was, lofty and thin,
Her ensign ruffling red, her bunts in pile,
Beauty and strength together, wonder, style.

DAUBER

"She docked close to the gates, and there she lay
Over the water from me, well in sight;
And as I worked I watched her all the day,
Finding her beauty ever fresh delight.
Her house-flag was bright green with strips of white;
High in the sunny air it rose to shake
Above the skysail poles most splendid rake."

"And when I felt unhappy I would look
Over the river at her, and her pride,
So calm, so quiet, came as a rebuke
To half the passionate pathways which I tried;
And though the autumn ran its term and died,
And winter fell and cold December came,
She was still splendid there, and still the same.

"Then on a day she sailed; but when she went
My mind was clear on what I had to try:
To see the sea and ships, and what they meant,
That was the thing I longed to do; so I
Drew and worked hard, and studied and put by,
And thought of nothing else but that one end,
But let all else go hang—love, money, friend.

DAUBER

" And now I've shipped as Dauber I've begun.
It was hard work to find a dauber's berth ;
I hadn't any friends to find me one,
Only my skill, for what it may be worth ;
But I'm at sea now, going about the earth,
And when the ship's paid off, when we return,
I'll join some Paris studio and learn."

He stopped, the air came moist, Si did not speak ;
The Dauber turned his eyes to where he sat,
Pressing the sail-room hinges with his cheek,
His face half covered with a drooping hat.
Huge dewdrops from the stay-sails dropped and spat.
Si did not stir, the Dauber touched his sleeve ;
A little birdlike noise came from a sheave.

Si was asleep, sleeping a calm deep sleep,
Still as a warden of the Egyptian dead
In some old haunted temple buried deep
Under the desert sand, sterile and red.
The Dauber shook his arm ; Si jumped and said,
" Good yarn, I swear !   I say, you have a brain—
Was that eight bells that went ?"   He slept again.

DAUBER

Then waking up, " I've had a nap," he cried.
" Was that one bell ?   What, Dauber, you still here ?"
"Si there ?" the Mate's voice called. "Sir," he replied.
The order made the lad's thick vision clear ;
A something in the Mate's voice made him fear.
" Si," said the Mate, " I hear you've made a friend—
Dauber, in short.   That friendship's got to end.

" You're a young gentleman.   Your place aboard
Is with the gentlemen abaft the mast.
You're learning to command ; you can't afford
To yarn with any man.   But there . . . it's past.
You've done it once ; let this time be the last.
The Dauber's place is forward.   Do it again,
I'll put you bunking forward with the men.

" Dismiss."   Si went, but Sam, beside the Mate,
Timekeeper there, walked with him to the rail
And whispered him the menace of " You wait "—
Words which have turned full many a reefer pale.
The watch was changed ; the watch on deck trimmed
    sail.
Sam, going below, called all the reefers down,
Sat in his bunk and eyed them with a frown.

DAUBER

"Si here," he said, "has soiled the half-deck's name
Talking to Dauber—Dauber, the ship's clout.
A reefer takes the Dauber for a flame,
The half-deck take the round-house walking out.
He's soiled the half-deck's honour ; now, no doubt,
The Bosun and his mates will come here sneaking,
Asking for smokes, or blocking gangways speaking.

"I'm not a vain man, given to blow or boast ;
I'm not a proud man, but I truly feel
That while I've bossed this mess and ruled this roast
I've kept this hooker's half-deck damned genteel.
Si must ask pardon, or be made to squeal.
Down on your knees, dog ; them we love we chasten.
Jao, pasea, my son—in English, Hasten."

Si begged for pardon, meekly kneeling down
Before the reefer's mess assembled grim.
The lamp above them smoked the glass all brown ;
Beyond the door the dripping sails were dim.
The Dauber passed the door ; none spoke to him.
He sought his berth and slept, or, waking, heard
Rain on the deck-house—rain, no other word.

IV

Out of the air a time of quiet came,
Calm fell upon the heaven like a drowth ;
The brass sky watched the brassy water flame.
Drowsed as a snail the clipper loitered south
Slowly, with no white bone across her mouth ;
No rushing glory, like a queen made bold,
The Dauber strove to draw her as she rolled.

There the four leaning spires of canvas rose,
Royals and skysails lifting, gently lifting,
White like the brightness that a great fish blows
When billows are at peace and ships are drifting ;
With mighty jerks that set the shadows shifting,
The courses tugged their tethers : a blue haze
Drifted like ghosts of flocks come down to graze.

DAUBER

There the great skyline made her perfect round,
Notched now and then by the sea's deeper blue ;
A smoke-smutch marked a steamer homeward bound,
The haze wrought all things to intenser hue.
In tingling impotence the Dauber drew
As all men draw, keen to the shaken soul
To give a hint that might suggest the whole.

A naked seaman washing a red shirt
Sat at a tub whistling between his teeth ;
Complaining blocks quavered like something hurt.
A sailor cut an old boot for a sheath,
The ship bowed to her shadow-ship beneath,
And little slaps of spray came at the roll
On to the deck-planks from the scupper-hole.

He watched it, painting patiently, as paints
With eyes that pierce behind the blue sky's veil,
The Benedictine in a Book of Saints
Watching the passing of the Holy Grail ;
The green dish dripping blood, the trump, the hail,
The spears that pass, the memory and the passion,
The beauty moving under this world's fashion.

40

DAUBER

But as he painted, slowly, man by man,
The seamen gathered near ; the Bosun stood
Behind him, jeering ; then the Sails began
Sniggering with comment that it was not good.
Chips flicked his sketch with little scraps of wood,
Saying, "That hit the top-knot," every time.
Cook mocked, " My lovely drawings ; it's a crime."

Slowly the men came nearer, till a crowd
Stood at his elbow, muttering as he drew ;
The Bosun, turning to them, spoke aloud,
" This is the ship that never got there.   You
Look at her here, what Dauber's trying to do.
Look at her ! lummy, like a Christmas-tree.
That thing's a ship ; he calls this painting.   See ?"

Seeing the crowd, the Mate came forward ; then
" Sir," said the Bosun, " come and see the sight !
Here's Dauber makes a circus for the men.
He calls this thing a ship—this hell's delight !"
" Man," said the Mate, " you'll never get her right
Daubing like that.   Look here !"   He took a brush.
" Now, Dauber, watch ; I'll put you to the blush.

41

DAUBER

" Look here.   Look there.   Now watch this ship of
         mine."
He drew her swiftly from a memory stored.
" God, sir," the Bosun said, " you do her fine !"
" Ay," said the Mate, " I do so, by the Lord !
I'll paint a ship with any man aboard."
They hung about his sketch like beasts at bait.
" There now, I taught him painting," said the Mate.

When he had gone, the gathered men dispersed ;
Yet two or three still lingered to dispute
What errors made the Dauber's work the worst.
They probed his want of knowledge to the root.
" Bei Gott !" they swore, " der Dauber cannot do 't ;
He haf no knolich how to put der pense.
Der Mate's is goot.   Der Dauber haf no sense."

" You hear ?" the Bosun cried, " you cannot do it !"
" A gospel truth," the Cook said, " true as hell !
And wisdom, Dauber, if you only knew it ;
A five year boy would do a ship as well."
" If that's the kind of thing you hope to sell,
God help you," echoed Chips.   " I tell you true,
The job's beyond you, Dauber ; drop it, do.

42

DAUBER

" Drop it, in God's name drop it, and have done !
You see you cannot do it.   Here's the Mate
Paints you to frazzles before everyone ;
Paints you a dandy clipper while you wait.
While you, Lord love us, daub.   I tell you straight,
We've had enough of daubing ; drop it ; quit.
You cannot paint, so make an end of it."

" That's sense," said all ; " you cannot, why pretend ?"
The Dauber rose and put his easel by.
" You've said enough," he said, " now let it end.
Who cares how bad my painting may be ?   I
Mean to go on, and, if I fail, to try.
However much I miss of my intent,
If I have done my best I'll be content.

" You cannot understand that.   Let it be.
You cannot understand, nor know, nor share.
This is a matter touching only me ;
My sketch may be a daub, for aught I care.
You may be right.   But even if you were,
Your mocking should not stop this work of mine ;
Rot though it be, its prompting is divine.

43

DAUBER

" You cannot understand that—you, and you,
And you, you Bosun. You can stand and jeer,
That is the task your spirit fits you to,
That you can understand and hold most dear.
Grin, then, like collars, ear to donkey ear,
But let me daub. Try, you, to understand
Which task will bear the light best on God's hand."

V

THE wester came as steady as the Trades;
Brightly it blew, and still the ship did shoulder
The brilliance of the water's white cockades
Into the milky green of smoky smoulder.
The sky grew bluer and the air grew colder.
Southward she thundered while the westers held,
Proud, with taut bridles, pawing, but compelled.

And still the Dauber strove, though all men mocked,
To draw the splendour of the passing thing,
And deep inside his heart a something locked,
Long pricking in him, now began to sting—
A fear of the disasters storm might bring;
His rank as painter would be ended then—
He would keep watch and watch like other men.

DAUBER

And go aloft with them to man the yard
When the great ship was rolling scuppers under,
Burying her snout all round the compass card,
While the green water struck at her and stunned her ;
When the lee-rigging slacked, when one long thunder
Boomed from the black to windward, when the sail
Booted and spurred the devil in the gale

For him to ride on men : that was the time
The Dauber dreaded ; then the test would come,
When seas, half-frozen, slushed the decks with slime,
And all the air was blind with flying scum ;
When the drenched sails were furled, when the fierce
    hum
In weather riggings died into the roar
Of God's eternal never tamed by shore.

Once in the passage he had worked aloft,
Shifting her suits one summer afternoon,
In the bright Trade wind, when the wind was soft,
Shaking the points, making the tackle croon.
But that was child's play to the future : soon
He would be ordered up when sails and spars
Were flying and going mad among the stars.

DAUBER

He had been scared that first time, daunted, thrilled,
Not by the height so much as by the size,
And then the danger to the man unskilled
In standing on a rope that runs through eyes.
" But in a storm," he thought, " the yards will rise
And roll together down, and snap their gear!"
The sweat came cold upon his palms for fear.

Sometimes in Gloucester he had felt a pang
Swinging below the house-eaves on a stage.
But stages carry rails; here he would hang
Upon a jerking rope in a storm's rage,
Ducked that the sheltering oilskin might assuage
The beating of the storm, clutching the jack,
Beating the sail, and being beaten back.

Drenched, frozen, gasping, blinded, beaten dumb,
High in the night, reeling great blinding arcs
As the ship rolled, his chappy fingers numb,
The deck below a narrow blur of marks,
The sea a welter of whiteness shot with sparks,
Now snapping up in bursts, now dying away,
Salting the horizontal snow with spray.

DAUBER

A hundred and fifty feet above the deck,
And there, while the ship rolls, boldly to sit
Upon a foot-rope moving, jerk and check,
While half a dozen seamen work on it;
Held by one hand, straining, by strength and wit
To toss a gasket's coil around the yard,
How could he compass that when blowing hard?

And if he failed in any least degree,
Or faltered for an instant, or showed slack,
He might go drown himself within the sea,
And add a bubble to the clipper's track.
He had signed his name, there was no turning back,
No pardon for default—this must be done.
One iron rule at sea binds everyone.

Till now he had been treated with contempt
As neither man nor thing, a creature borne
On the ship's articles, but left exempt
From all the seamen's life except their scorn.
But he would rank as seaman off the Horn,
Work as a seaman, and be kept or cast
By standards set for men before the mast.

48

DAUBER

Even now they shifted suits of sails; they bent
The storm-suit ready for the expected time;
The mighty wester that the Plate had lent
Had brought them far into the wintry clime.
At dawn, out of the shadow, there was rime,
The dim Magellan Clouds were frosty clear,
The wind had edge, the testing-time was near.

And then he wondered if the tales were lies
Told by old hands to terrify the new,
For, since the ship left England, only twice
Had there been need to start a sheet or clew,
Then only royals, for an hour or two,
And no seas broke aboard, nor was it cold.
What were these gales of which the stories told?

The thought went by. He had heard the Bosun tell
Too often, and too fiercely, not to know
That being off the Horn in June is hell:
Hell of continual toil in ice and snow,
Frostbitten hell in which the westers blow
Shrieking for days on end, in which the seas
Gulf the starved seamen till their marrows freeze.

DAUBER

Such was the weather he might look to find,
Such was the work expected : there remained
Firmly to set his teeth, resolve his mind,
And be the first, however much it pained,
And bring his honour round the Horn unstained,
And win his mates' respect ; and thence, untainted,
Be ranked as man however much he painted.

He drew deep breath ; a gantline swayed aloft
A lower topsail, hard with rope and leather,
Such as men's frozen fingers fight with oft
Below the Ramirez in Cape Horn weather.
The arms upon the yard hove all together,
Lighting the head along ; a thought occurred
Within the painter's brain like a bright bird :

That this, and so much like it, of man's toil,
Compassed by naked manhood in strange places,
Was all heroic, but outside the coil
Within which modern art gleams or grimaces ;
That if he drew that line of sailors' faces
Sweating the sail, their passionate play and change,
It would be new, and wonderful, and strange.

DAUBER

That that was what his work meant; it would be
A training in new vision—a revealing
Of passionate men in battle with the sea,
High on an unseen stage, shaking and reeling;
And men through him would understand their feeling,
Their might, their misery, their tragic power,
And all by suffering pain a little hour;

High on the yard with them, feeling their pain,
Battling with them; and it had not been done.
He was a door to new worlds in the brain,
A window opening letting in the sun,
A voice saying, "Thus is bread fetched and ports won,
And life lived out at sea where men exist
Solely by man's strong brain and sturdy wrist."

So he decided, as he cleaned his brasses,
Hearing without, aloft, the curse, the shout
Where the taut gantline passes and repasses,
Heaving new topsails to be lighted out.
It was most proud, however self might doubt,
To share man's tragic toil and paint it true.
He took the offered Fate: this he would do.

51

DAUBER

That night the snow fell between six and seven,
A little feathery fall so light, so dry—
An aimless dust out of a confused heaven,
Upon an air no steadier than a sigh ;
The powder dusted down and wandered by
So purposeless, so many, and so cold,
Then died, and the wind ceased and the ship rolled.

Rolled till she clanged—rolled till the brain was tired,
Marking the acme of the heaves, the pause
While the sea-beauty rested and respired,
Drinking great draughts of roller at her hawse.
Flutters of snow came aimless upon flaws.
"Lock up your paints," the Mate said, speaking light :
"This is the Horn ; you'll join my watch to-night !"

VI

ALL through the windless night the clipper rolled
In a great swell with oily gradual heaves
Which rolled her down until her time-bells tolled,
Clang, and the weltering water moaned like beeves.
The thundering rattle of slatting shook the sheaves,
Startles of water made the swing ports gush,
The sea was moaning and sighing and saying "Hush!"

It was all black and starless.   Peering down
Into the water, trying to pierce the gloom,
One saw a dim, smooth, oily glitter of brown
Heaving and dying away and leaving room
For yet another.   Like the march of doom
Came those great powers of marching silences;
Then fog came down, dead-cold, and hid the seas.

53

DAUBER

They set the Dauber to the foghorn.   There
He stood upon the poop, making to sound
Out of the pump the sailors' nasal blare,
Listening lest ice should make the note resound.
She bayed there like a solitary hound
Lost in a covert; all the watch she bayed.
The fog, come closelier down, no answer made.

Denser it grew, until the ship was lost.
The elemental hid her; she was merged
In mufflings of dark death, like a man's ghost,
New to the change of death, yet thither urged.
Then from the hidden waters something surged—
Mournful, despairing, great, greater than speech,
A noise like one slow wave on a still beach.

Mournful, and then again mournful, and still
Out of the night that mighty voice arose;
The Dauber at his foghorn felt the thrill.
Who rode that desolate sea?   What forms were those?
Mournful, from things defeated, in the throes
Of memory of some conquered hunting-ground,
Out of the night of death arose the sound.

DAUBER

"Whales!" said the mate. They stayed there all
    night long
Answering the horn.   Out of the night they spoke,
Defeated creatures who had suffered wrong,
But were still noble underneath the stroke.
They filled the darkness when the Dauber woke ;
The men came peering to the rail to hear,
And the sea sighed, and the fog rose up sheer.

A wall of nothing at the world's last edge,
Where no life came except defeated life.
The Dauber felt shut in within a hedge,
Behind which form was hidden and thought was rife,
And that a blinding flash, a thrust, a knife
Would sweep the hedge away and make all plain,
Brilliant beyond all words, blinding the brain.

So the night past, but then no morning broke—
Only a something showed that night was dead.
A sea-bird, cackling like a devil, spoke,
And the fog drew away and hung like lead.
Like mighty cliffs it shaped, sullen and red ;
Like glowering gods at watch it did appear,
And sometimes drew away, and then drew near.

DAUBER

Like islands, and like chasms, and like hell,
But always mighty and red, gloomy and ruddy,
Shutting the visible sea in like a well;
Slow heaving in vast ripples, blank and muddy,
Where the sun should have risen it streaked bloody.
The day was still-born; all the sea-fowl scattering
Splashed the still water, mewing, hovering, clattering.

Then Polar snow came down little and light,
Till all the sky was hidden by the small,
Most multitudinous drift of dirty white
Tumbling and wavering down and covering all—
Covering the sky, the sea, the clipper tall,
Furring the ropes with white, casing the mast,
Coming on no known air, but blowing past.

And all the air seemed full of gradual moan,
As though in those cloud-chasms the horns were
    blowing
The mort for gods cast out and overthrown,
Or for the eyeless sun plucked out and going.
Slow the low gradual moan came in the snowing;
The Dauber felt the prelude had begun.
The snowstorm fluttered by; he saw the sun

DAUBER

Show and pass by, gleam from one towering prison
Into another, vaster and more grim,
Which in dull crags of darkness had arisen
To muffle-to a final door on him.
The gods upon the dull crags lowered dim,
The pigeons chattered, quarrelling in the track.
In the south-west the dimness dulled to black.

Then came the cry of "Call all hands on deck!"
The Dauber knew its meaning; it was come:
Cape Horn, that tramples beauty into wreck,
And crumples steel and smites the strong man dumb.
Down clattered flying kites and staysails: some
Sang out in quick, high calls; the fairleads skirled,
And from the south-west came the end of the world.

"Caught in her ball-dress," said the Bosun, hauling;
"Lee-ay, lee-ay!" quick, high, came the men's call;
It was all wallop of sails and startled calling.
"Let fly!" "Let go!" "Clew up!" and "Let go all!"
"Now up and make them fast!" "Here, give us a
    haul!"
"Now up and stow them! Quick! By God! we're
    done!"
The blackness crunched all memory of the sun.

DAUBER

"Up!" said the Mate. "Mizen topgallants. Hurry!"
The Dauber ran, the others ran, the sails
Slatted and shook ; out of the black a flurry
Whirled in fine lines, tattering the edge to trails.
Painting and art and England were old tales
Told in some other life to that pale man,
Who struggled with white fear and gulped and ran.

He struck a ringbolt in his haste and fell—
Rose, sick with pain, half-lamed in his left knee ;
He reached the shrouds where clambering men pell-
    mell
Hustled each other up and cursed him ; he
Hurried aloft with them : then from the sea
Came a cold, sudden breath that made the hair
Stiff on the neck, as though Death whispered there.

A man below him punched him in the side.
"Get up, you Dauber, or let me get past."
He saw the belly of the skysail skied,
Gulped, and clutched tight, and tried to go more fast.
Sometimes he missed his ratline and was grassed,
Scraped his shin raw against the rigid line.
The clamberers reached the futtock-shrouds' incline.

DAUBER

Cursing they came; one, kicking out behind,
Kicked Dauber in the mouth, and one below
Punched at his calves; the futtock-shrouds inclined,
It was a perilous path for one to go.
" Up, Dauber, up!"   A curse followed a blow.
He reached the top and gasped, then on, then on.
And one voice yelled " Let go !" and one " All gone !"

Fierce clamberers, some in oilskins, some in rags,
Hustling and hurrying up, up the steep stairs.
Before the windless sails were blown to flags,
And whirled like dirty birds athwart great airs,
Ten men in all, to get this mast of theirs
Snugged to the gale in time. " Up ! Damn you, run !"
The mizen topmast head was safely won.

" Lay out !" the Bosun yelled.   The Dauber laid
Out on the yard, gripping the yard, and feeling
Sick at the mighty space of air displayed
Below his feet, where mewing birds were wheeling.
A giddy fear was on him ; he was reeling.
He bit his lip half through, clutching the jack.
A cold sweat glued the shirt upon his back.

59

DAUBER

The yard was shaking, for a brace was loose.
He felt that he would fall; he clutched, he bent,
Clammy with natural terror to the shoes
While idiotic promptings came and went.
Snow fluttered on a wind-flaw and was spent;
He saw the water darken.   Someone yelled,
" Frap it; don't stay to furl !   Hold on !"   He held.

Darkness came down—half darkness—in a whirl;
The sky went out, the waters disappeared.
He felt a shocking pressure of blowing hurl
The ship upon her side.   The darkness speared
At her with wind; she staggered, she careered,
Then down she lay.   The Dauber felt her go;
He saw his yard tilt downwards.   Then the snow

Whirled all about—dense, multitudinous, cold—
Mixed with the wind's one devilish thrust and shriek,
Which whiffled out men's tears, deafened, took hold,
Flattening the flying drift against the cheek.
The yards buckled and bent, man could not speak.
The ship lay on her broadside; the wind's sound
Had devilish malice at having got her downed.

*   *   *   *   *

DAUBER

How long the gale had blown he could not tell,
Only the world had changed, his life had died.
A moment now was everlasting hell.
Nature an onslaught from the weather side,
A withering rush of death, a frost that cried,
Shrieked, till he withered at the heart ; a hail
Plastered his oilskins with an icy mail.

"Cut!" yelled his mate. He looked—the sail was gone,
Blown into rags in the first furious squall ;
The tatters drummed the devil's tattoo.   On
The buckling yard a block thumped like a mall.
The ship lay—the sea smote her, the wind's bawl
Came, " loo, loo, loo !"   The devil cried his hounds
On to the poor spent stag strayed in his bounds.

"Cut ! Ease her !" yelled his mate; the Dauber heard.
His mate wormed up the tilted yard and slashed,
A rag of canvas skimmed like a darting bird.
The snow whirled, the ship bowed to it, the gear
    lashed,
The sea tops were cut off and flung down smashed ;
Tatters of shouts were flung, the rags of yells—
And clang, clang, clang, below beat the two bells.

61

DAUBER

" O God !" the Dauber moaned.   A roaring rang,
Blasting the royals like a cannonade ;
The backstays parted with a cracking clang,
The upper spars were snapped like twigs decayed —
Snapped at their heels, their jagged splinters splayed,
Like white and ghastly hair erect with fear.
The Mate yelled, " Gone, by God, and pitched
    them clear !"

" Up !" yelled the bosun ; " up and clear the wreck !"
The Dauber followed where he led : below
He caught one giddy glimpsing of the deck
Filled with white water, as though heaped with snow.
He saw the streamers of the rigging blow
Straight out like pennons from the splintered mast,
Then, all sense dimmed, all was an icy blast

Roaring from nether hell and filled with ice,
Roaring and crashing on the jerking stage,
An utter bridle given to utter vice,
Limitless power mad with endless rage
Withering the soul ; a minute seemed an age.
He clutched and hacked at ropes, at rags of sail,
Thinking that comfort was a fairy-tale

DAUBER

Told long ago—long, long ago—long since
Heard of in other lives—imagined, dreamed—
There where the basest beggar was a prince
To him in torment where the tempest screamed,
Comfort and warmth and ease no longer seemed
Things that a man could know : soul, body, brain,
Knew nothing but the wind, the cold, the pain.

"Leave that !" the Bosun shouted ; "Crojick save !"
The splitting crojick, not yet gone to rags,
Thundered below, beating till something gave,
Bellying between its buntlines into bags.
Some birds were blown past, shrieking : dark, like shags,
Their backs seemed, looking down.   "Leu, leu !"
    they cried.
The ship lay, the seas thumped her ; she had died.

They reached the crojick yard, which buckled, buckled
Like a thin whalebone to the topsail's strain.
They laid upon the yard and heaved and knuckled,
Pounding the sail, which jangled and leapt again.
It was quite hard with ice, its rope like chain,
Its strength like seven devils ; it shook the mast.
They cursed and toiled and froze : a long time passed.

63

DAUBER

Two hours passed, then a dim lightening came.
Those frozen ones upon the yard could see
The mainsail and the foresail still the same,
Still battling with the hands and blowing free,
Rags tattered where the staysails used to be.
The lower topsails stood; the ship's lee deck
Seethed with four feet of water filled with wreck.

An hour more went by; the Dauber lost
All sense of hands and feet, all sense of all
But of a wind that cut him to the ghost,
And of a frozen fold he had to haul,
Of heavens that fell and never ceased to fall,
And ran in smoky snatches along the sea,
Leaping from crest to wave-crest, yelling.   He

Lost sense of time; no bells went, but he felt
Ages go over him.   At last, at last
They frapped the cringled crojick's icy pelt;
In frozen bulge and bunt they made it fast.
Then, scarcely live, they laid in to the mast.
The Captain's speaking-trumpet gave a blare,
" Make fast the topsail, Mister, while you're there."

64

DAUBER

Some seamen cursed, but up they had to go—
Up to the topsail yard to spend an hour
Stowing a topsail in a blinding snow,
Which made the strongest man among them cower.
More men came up, the fresh hands gave them power,
They stowed the sail; then with a rattle of chain
One half the crojick burst its bonds again.

  *   *   *   *   *

They stowed the sail, frapping it round with rope,
Leaving no surface for the wind, no fold,
Then down the weather-shrouds, half dead, they grope;
That struggle with the sail had made them old.
They wondered if the crojick furl would hold.
" Lucky," said one, " it didn't spring the spar."
" Lucky," the Bosun said, " lucky !   We are !

She came within two shakes of turning top
Or stripping all her shroud-screws, that first quiff.
Now fish those wash-deck buckets out of the slop.
Here's Dauber says he doesn't like Cape Stiff.
This isn't wind, man, this is only a whiff.
Hold on, all hands, hold on !" a sea, half seen,
Paused, mounted, burst, and filled the main-deck green.

DAUBER

The Dauber felt a mountain of water fall.
It covered him deep, deep, he felt it fill,
Over his head, the deck, the fife-rails, all,
Quieting the ship, she trembled and lay still.
Then with a rush and shatter and clanging shrill
Over she went; he saw the water cream
Over the bitts; he saw the half-deck stream.

Then in the rush he swirled, over she went;
Her lee-rail dipped, he struck, and something gave;
His legs went through a port as the roll spent;
She paused, then rolled, and back the water drave.
He drifted with it as a part of the wave,
Drowning, half-stunned, exhausted, partly frozen,
He struck the booby hatchway; then the Bosun

Leaped, seeing his chance, before the next sea burst,
And caught him as he drifted, seized him, held,
Up-ended him against the bitts, and cursed.
"This ain't the George's Swimming Baths," he yelled;
" Keep on your feet!"   Another grey-back felled
The two together, and the Bose, half-blind,
Spat : "One's a joke," he cursed, " but two's unkind."

66

DAUBER

" Now, damn it, Dauber!" said the Mate. " Look out,
Or you'll be over the side !" The water freed ;
Each clanging freeing-port became a spout.
The men cleared up the decks as there was need.
The Dauber's head was cut, he felt it bleed
Into his oilskins as he clutched and coiled.
Water and sky were devils' brews which boiled,

Boiled, shrieked, and glowered; but the ship was saved.
Snugged safely down, though fourteen sails were
    split.
Out of the dark a fiercer fury raved.
The grey-backs died and mounted, each crest lit
With a white toppling gleam that hissed from it
And slid, or leaped, or ran with whirls of cloud,
Mad with inhuman life that shrieked aloud.

The watch was called ; Dauber might go below.
" Splice the main brace !" the Mate called. All laid aft
To get a gulp of momentary glow
As some reward for having saved the craft.
The steward ladled mugs, from which each quaff'd
Whisky, with water, sugar, and lime-juice, hot,
A quarter of a pint each made the tot.

DAUBER

Beside the lamp-room door the steward stood
Ladling it out, and each man came in turn,
Tipped his sou'-wester, drank it, grunted "Good!"
And shambled forward, letting it slowly burn.
When all were gone the Dauber lagged astern,
Torn by his frozen body's lust for heat,
The liquor's pleasant smell, so warm, so sweet,

And by a promise long since made at home
Never to taste strong liquor.   Now he knew
The worth of liquor; now he wanted some.
His frozen body urged him to the brew;
Yet it seemed wrong, an evil thing to do
To break that promise.   "Dauber," said the Mate,
"Drink, and turn in, man; why the hell d'ye wait?"

"Please, sir, I'm temperance."   "Temperance are
        you, hey?
That's all the more for me!   So you're for slops?
I thought you'd had enough slops for to-day.
Go to your bunk and ease her when she drops.
And—damme, steward! you brew with two much hops!
Stir up the sugar, man!—and tell your girl
How kind the Mate was teaching you to furl."

DAUBER

Then the Mate drank the remnants, six men's share,
And ramped into his cabin, where he stripped
And danced unclad, and was uproarious there.
In waltzes with the cabin cat he tripped,
Singing in tenor clear that he was pipped—
That "he who strove the tempest to disarm,
Must never first embrail the lee yard-arm,"

And that his name was Ginger.   Dauber crept
Back to the round-house, gripping by the rail.
The wind howled by ; the passionate water leapt ;
The night was all one roaring with the gale.
Then at the door he stopped, uttering a wail ;
His hands were perished numb and blue as veins,
He could not turn the knob for both the Spains.

A hand came shuffling aft, dodging the seas,
Singing " her nut-brown hair " between his teeth ;
Taking the ocean's tumult at his ease
Even when the wash about his thighs did seethe.
His soul was happy in its happy sheath ;
" What, Dauber, won't it open ?   Fingers cold ?
You'll talk of this time, Dauber, when you're old."

DAUBER

He flung the door half open, and a sea
Washed them both in, over the splashboard, down;
"You silly, salt miscarriage !" sputtered he.
"Dauber, pull out the plug before we drown !
That's spoiled my laces and my velvet gown.
Where is the plug?"   Groping in pitch dark water,
He sang between his teeth "The Farmer's Daughter."

It was pitch dark within there; at each roll
The chests slid to the slant; the water rushed,
Making full many a clanging tin pan bowl
Into the black below-bunks as it gushed.
The dog-tired men slept through it; they were hushed.
The water drained, and then with matches damp
The man struck heads off till he lit the lamp.

"Thank you," the Dauber said; the seaman grinned.
"This is your first foul weather ?" "Yes." "I thought
Up on the yard you hadn't seen much wind.
Them's rotten sea-boots, Dauber, that you brought.
Now I must cut on deck before I'm caught."
He went; the lamp-flame smoked; he slammed the
    door;
A film of water loitered across the floor.

DAUBER

The Dauber watched it come and watched it go ;
He had had revelation of the lies
Cloaking the truth men never choose to know ;
He could bear witness now and cleanse their eyes.
He had beheld in suffering ; he was wise ;
This was the sea, this searcher of the soul—
This never-dying shriek fresh from the Pole.

He shook with cold ; his hands could not undo
His oilskin buttons, so he shook and sat,
Watching his dirty fingers, dirty blue,
Hearing without the hammering tackle slat,
Within, the drops from dripping clothes went pat,
Running in little patters, gentle, sweet,
And " Ai, ai !" went the wind, and the seas beat.

His bunk was sopping wet ; he clambered in.
None of his clothes were dry ; his fear recurred.
Cramps bunched the muscles underneath his skin.
The great ship rolled until the lamp was blurred.
He took his Bible and tried to read a word ;
Trembled at going aloft again, and then
Resolved to fight it out and show it to men.

DAUBER

Faces recurred, fierce memories of the yard,
The frozen sail, the savage eyes, the jests,
The oaths of one great seaman syphilis-scarred,
The tug of leeches jammed beneath their chests,
The buntlines bellying bunts out into breasts.
The deck so desolate-grey, the sky so wild,
He fell asleep, and slept like a young child.

But not for long; the cold awoke him soon,
The hot-ache and the skin-cracks and the cramp,
The seas thundering without, the gale's wild tune,
The sopping misery of the blankets damp.
A speaking-trumpet roared; a sea-boot's stamp
Clogged at the door.   A man entered to shout:
" All hands on deck !   Arouse here !   Tumble out !"

The caller raised the lamp; his oilskins clicked
As the thin ice upon them cracked and fell.
" Rouse out !" he said.   " This lamp is frozen wicked.
Rouse out !"   His accent deepened to a yell.
" We're among ice ; it's blowing up like hell.
We're going to hand both topsails.   Time, I guess,
We're sheeted up.   Rouse out !   Don't stay to dress !"

DAUBER

" Is it cold on deck ?" said Dauber.   " Is it cold ?
We're sheeted up, I tell you, inches thick !
The fo'c'sle's like a wedding-cake, I'm told.
Now tumble out, my sons ; on deck here, quick !
Rouse out, away, and come and climb the stick.
I'm going to call the half-deck.   Bosun ! Hey !
Both topsails coming in.   Heave out ! Away !"

He went ; the Dauber tumbled from his bunk,
Clutching the side.   He heard the wind go past,
Making the great ship wallow as if drunk.
There was a shocking tumult up the mast.
" This is the end," he muttered, " come at last !
I've got to go aloft, facing this cold.
I can't.   I can't.   I'll never keep my hold.

" I cannot face the topsail yard again.
I never guessed what misery it would be."
The cramps and hot-ache made him sick with pain.
The ship stopped suddenly from a devilish sea,
Then, with a triumph of wash, a rush of glee,
The door burst in, and in the water rolled,
Filling the lower bunks, black, creaming, cold.

73

DAUBER

The lamp sucked out. "Wash!" went the water back,
Then in again, flooding; the Bosun swore.
"You useless thing! You Dauber! You lee slack
Get out, you heekapoota! Shut the door!
You coo-ilyaira, what are you waiting for?
Out of my way, you thing—you useless thing!"
He slammed the door indignant, clanging the ring.

And then he lit the lamp, drowned to the waist;
"Here's a fine house! Get at the scupper-holes"—
He bent against it as the water raced—
"And pull them out to leeward when she rolls.
They say some kinds of landsmen don't have souls.
I well believe. A Port Mahon baboon
Would make more soul than you got with a spoon."

Down in the icy water Dauber groped
To find the plug; the racing water sluiced
Over his head and shoulders as she sloped.
Without, judged by the sound, all hell was loosed.
He felt cold Death about him tightly noosed.
That Death was better than the misery there
Iced on the quaking foothold high in air.

DAUBER

And then the thought came : " I'm a failure.   All
My life has been a failure.   They were right.
It will not matter if I go and fall ;
I should be free then from this hell's delight.
I'll never paint.   Best let it end to-night.
I'll slip over the side.   I've tried and failed."
So in the ice-cold in the night he quailed.

Death would be better, death, than this long hell
Of mockery and surrender and dismay—
This long defeat of doing nothing well,
Playing the part too high for him to play.
" O Death ! who hides the sorry thing away,
Take me ; I've failed.   I cannot play these cards."
There came a thundering from the topsail yards.

And then he bit his lips, clenching his mind,
And staggered out to muster, beating back
The coward frozen self of him that whined.
Come what cards might he meant to play the pack.
"Ai!" screamed the wind ; the topsail sheets went
      clack ;
Ice filled the air with spikes ; the grey-backs burst.
" Here's Dauber," said the Mate, "on deck the first.

DAUBER

" Why, holy sailor, Dauber, you're a man !
I took you for a soldier.   Up now, come !"
Up on the yards already they began
That battle with a gale which strikes men dumb.
The leaping topsail thundered like a drum.
The frozen snow beat in the face like shots.
The wind spun whipping wave-crests into clots.

So up upon the topsail yard again,
In the great tempest's fiercest hour, began
Probation to the Dauber's soul, of pain
Which crowds a century's torment in a span.
For the next month the ocean taught this man,
And he, in that month's torment, while she wested,
Was never warm nor dry, nor full nor rested.

But still it blew, or, if it lulled, it rose
Within the hour and blew again ; and still
The water as it burst aboard her froze.
The wind blew off an ice-field, raw and chill,
Daunting man's body, tampering with his will ;
But after thirty days a ghostly sun
Gave sickly promise that the storms were done.

VII

A GREAT grey sea was running up the sky,
Desolate birds flew past; their mewings came
As that lone water's spiritual cry,
Its forlorn voice, its essence, its soul's name.
The ship limped in the water as if lame.
Then in the forenoon watch to a great shout
More sail was made, the reefs were shaken out.

A slant came from the south; the singers stood
Clapped to the halliards, hauling to a tune,
Old as the sea, a fillip to the blood.
The upper topsail rose like a balloon.
"So long, Cape Stiff.   In Valparaiso soon,"
Said one to other, as the ship lay over,
Making her course again—again a rover.

DAUBER

Slowly the sea went down as the wind fell.
Clear rang the songs, " Hurrah ! Cape Horn is bet !"
The combless seas were lumping into swell ;
The leaking fo'c'sles were no longer wet.
More sail was made ; the watch on deck was set
To cleaning up the ruin broken bare
Below, aloft, about her, everywhere.

The Dauber, scrubbing out the round-house, found
Old pantiles pulped among the mouldy gear,
Washed underneath the bunks and long since drowned
During the agony of the Cape Horn year.
He sang in scrubbing, for he had done with fear—
Fronted the worst and looked it in the face ;
He had got manhood at the testing-place.

Singing he scrubbed, passing his watch below,
Making the round-house fair ; the Bosun watched,
Bringing his knitting slowly to the toe.
Sails stretched a mizen skysail which he patched ;
They thought the Dauber was a bad egg hatched.
" Daubs," said the Bosun cheerly, " can you knit ?
I've made a Barney's bull of this last bit."

DAUBER

Then, while the Dauber counted, Bosun took
Some marline from his pocket. " Here," he said,
" You want to know square sennit? So fash. Look !
Eight foxes take, and stop the ends with thread.
I've known an engineer would give his head
To know square sennit."   As the Rose began,
The Dauber felt promoted into man.

It was his warrant that he had not failed—
That the most hard part in his difficult climb
Had not been past attainment; it was scaled :
Safe footing showed above the slippery slime.
He had emerged out of the iron time,
And knew that he could compass his life's scheme ;
He had the power sufficient to his dream.

Then dinner came, and now the sky was blue.
The ship was standing north, the Horn was rounded ;
She made a thundering as she weltered through.
The mighty grey-backs glittered as she bounded.
More sail was piled upon her ; she was hounded
North, while the wind came ; like a stag she ran
Over grey hills and hollows of seas wan.

79

DAUBER

She had a white bone in her mouth : she sped ;
Those in the round-house watched her as they ate
Their meal of pork-fat fried with broken bread.
"Good old!" they cried.   "She's off; she's gathering
    gait !"
Her track was whitening like a Lammas spate.
"Good old!" they cried. "Oh, give her cloth! Hurray!
For three weeks more to Valparaiso Bay !"

" She smells old Vallipo," the Bosun cried.
" We'll be inside the tier in three weeks more,
Lying at double-moorings where they ride
Off of the market, half a mile from shore,
And bumboat pan, my sons, and figs galore,
And girls in black mantillas fit to make a
Poor seaman frantic when they dance the cueca."

Eight bells were made, the watch was changed, and now
The Mate spoke to the Dauber : " This is better.
We'll soon be getting mudhooks over the bow.
She'll make her passage still if this'll let her.
Oh, run, you drogher ! dip your fo'c'sle wetter.
Well, Dauber, this is better than Cape Horn.
Them topsails made you wish you'd not been born.

DAUBER

" Yes, sir," the Dauber said.   " Now," said the Mate,
" We've got to smart her up.   Them Cape Horn seas
Have made her paint-work like a rusty grate.
Oh, didn't them topsails make your fish-hooks freeze ?
A topsail don't pay heed to ' Won't you, please ?'
Well, you have seen Cape Horn, my son ; you've learned.
You've dipped your hand and had your fingers burned.

" And now you'll stow that folly, trying to paint.
You've had your lesson ; you're a sailor now.
You come on board a female ripe to faint.
All sorts of slush you'd learned, the Lord knows how.
Cape Horn has sent you wisdom over the bow
If you've got sense to take it.   You're a sailor.
My God ! before you were a woman's tailor.

" So throw your paints to blazes and have done.
Words can't describe the silly things you did
Sitting before your easel in the sun,
With all your colours on the paint-box lid.
I blushed for you . . . and then the daubs you hid.
My God ! you'll have more sense now, eh ?   You've
    quit ?"
"No, sir."   "You've not ?"   "No, sir."   "God give you
    wit.

DAUBER

"I thought you'd come to wisdom." Thus they talked,
While the great clipper took her bit and rushed
Like a skin-glistening stallion not yet baulked,
Till fire-bright water at her swing-ports gushed ;
Poising and bowing down her fore-foot crushed
Bubble on glittering bubble ; on she went.
The Dauber watched her, wondering what it meant.

To come, after long months, at rosy dawn,
Into the placid blue of some great bay.
Treading the quiet water like a fawn
Ere yet the morning haze was blown away.
A rose-flushed figure putting by the grey,
And anchoring there before the city smoke
Rose, or the church-bells rang, or men awoke.

And then, in the first light, to see grow clear
That long-expected haven filled with strangers—
Alive with men and women ; see and hear
Its clattering market and its money-changers ;
And hear the surf beat, and be free from dangers,
And watch the crinkled ocean blue with calm
Drowsing beneath the Trade, beneath the palm.

82

DAUBER

Hungry for that he worked ; the hour went by,
And still the wind grew, still the clipper strode,
And now a darkness hid the western sky,
And sprays came flicking off at the wind's goad.
She stumbled now, feeling her sail a load.
The Mate gazed hard to windward, eyed his sail,
And said the Horn was going to flick her tail.

Boldly he kept it on her till she staggered,
But still the wind increased ; it grew, it grew,
Darkening the sky, making the water haggard ;
Full of small snow the mighty wester blew.
"More fun for little fish-hooks," sighed the crew.
They eyed the taut topgallants stiff like steel ;
A second hand was ordered to the wheel.

The Captain eyed her aft, sucking his lip,
Feeling the sail too much, but yet refraining
From putting hobbles on the leaping ship,
The glad sea-shattering stallion, halter-straining,
Wind-musical, uproarious, and complaining ;
But, in a gust, he cocked his finger, so :
"You'd better take them off, before they go."

DAUBER

All saw.   They ran at once without the word
" Leeay !   Leeay !"   Loud rang the clew-line cries ;
Sam in his bunk within the half-deck heard,
Stirred in his sleep, and rubbed his drowsy eyes.
" There go the lower to'gallants."   Against the skies
Rose the thin bellying strips of leaping sail.
The Dauber was the first man over the rail.

Three to a mast they ran ; it was a race.
" God !" said the Mate ; " that Dauber, he can go."
He watched the runners with an upturned face
Over the futtocks, struggling heel to toe,
Up to the topmast cross-trees into the blow
Where the three sails were leaping.   " Dauber
        wins !"
The yards were reached, and now the race begins.

Which three will furl their sail first and come down ?
Out to the yard-arm for the leech goes one,
His hair blown flagwise from a hatless crown,
His hands at work like fever to be done.
Out of the gale a fiercer fury spun.
The three sails leaped together, yanking high,
Like talons darting up to clutch the sky.

DAUBER

The Dauber on the fore-topgallant yard
Out at the weather yard-arm was the first
To lay his hand upon the buntline-barred
Topgallant yanking to the wester's burst ;
He craned to catch the leech ; his comrades cursed ;
One at the buntlines, one with oaths observed,
" The eye of the outer jib-stay isn't served."

" No," said the Dauber.   " No," the man replied.
They heaved, stowing the sail, not looking round,
Panting, but full of life and eager-eyed ;
The gale roared at them with its iron sound.
" That's you," the Dauber said.   His gasket wound
Swift round the yard, binding the sail in bands ;
.There came a gust, the sail leaped from his hands,

So that he saw it high above him, grey,
And there his mate was falling ; quick he clutched
An arm in oilskins swiftly snatched away.
A voice said " Christ !" a quick shape stooped and
    touched,
Chain struck his hands, ropes shot, the sky was
    smutched
With vast black fires that ran, that fell, that furled,
And then he saw the mast, the small snow hurled,

DAUBER

The fore-topgallant yard far, far aloft,
And blankness settling on him and great pain ;
And snow beneath his fingers wet and soft,
And topsail-sheet-blocks shaking at the chain.
He knew it was he who had fallen ; then his brain
Swirled in a circle while he watched the sky.
Infinite multitudes of snow blew by.

" I thought it was Tom who fell," his brain's voice said.
" Down on the bloody deck !" the Captain screamed.
The multitudinous little snow-flakes sped.
His pain was real enough, but all else seemed.
Si with a bucket ran, the water gleamed
Tilting upon him ; others came, the Mate . . .
They knelt with eager eyes like things that wait

For other things to come.   He saw them there.
" It will go on," he murmured, watching Si.
Colours and sounds seemed mixing in the air,
The pain was stunning him, and the wind went by.
" More water," said the Mate.   " Here, Bosun, try.
Ask if he's got a message.   Hell, he's gone !
Here, Dauber, paints."   He said, " It will go on."

DAUBER

Not knowing his meaning rightly, but he spoke
With the intenseness of a fading soul
Whose share of Nature's fire turns to smoke,
Whose hand on Nature's wheel loses control.
The eager faces glowered red like coal.
They glowed, the great storm glowed, the sails, the
      mast.
" It will go on," he cried aloud, and passed.

Those from the yard came down to tell the tale.
" He almost had me off," said Tom. " He slipped.
There come one hell of a jump-like from the sail. . . .
He clutched at me and almost had me pipped.
He caught my 'ris'band, but the oilskin ripped. . . .
It tore clean off. Look here. I was near gone.
I made a grab to catch him ; so did John.

" I caught his arm. My God ! I was near done.
He almost had me over ; it was near.
He hit the ropes and grabbed at every one."
" Well," said the Mate, " we cannot leave him here.
Run, Si, and get the half-deck table clear.
We'll lay him there. Catch hold there, you, and you.
He's dead, poor son ; there's nothing more to do."

DAUBER

Night fell, and all night long the Dauber lay
Covered upon the table ; all night long
The pitiless storm exulted at her prey,
Huddling the waters with her icy thong.
But to the covered shape she did no wrong.
He lay beneath the sailcloth.   Bell by bell
The night wore through; the stars rose, the stars fell.

Blowing most pitiless cold out of clear sky
The wind roared all night long ; and all night through
The green seas on the deck went washing by,
Flooding the half-deck ; bitter hard it blew.
But little of it all the Dauber knew—
The sopping bunks, the floating chests, the wet,
The darkness, and the misery, and the sweat.

He was off duty.   So it blew all night,
And when the watches changed the men would come
Dripping within the door to strike a light
And stare upon the Dauber lying dumb,
And say, " He come a cruel thump, poor chum."
Or, " He'd a-been a fine big man ;" or, " He . . .
A smart young seaman he was getting to be."

DAUBER

Or, " Damn it all, it's what we've all to face! . . .
I knew another fellow one time . . ." then
Came a strange tale of death in a strange place
Out on the sea, in ships, with wandering men.
In many ways Death puts us into pen.
The reefers came down tired and looked and slept.
Below the skylight little dribbles crept

Along the painted woodwork, glistening, slow,
Following the roll and dripping, never fast,
But dripping on the quiet form below,
Like passing time talking to time long past.
And all night long " Ai, ai !" went the wind's blast,
And creaming water swished below the pale,
Unheeding body stretched beneath the sail.

At dawn they sewed him up, and at eight bells
They bore him to the gangway, wading deep,
Through the green-clutching, white-toothed water-
    hells
That flung his carriers over in their sweep.
They laid an old red ensign on the heap,
And all hands stood bare-headed, stooping, swaying,
Washed by the sea while the old man was praying

DAUBER

Out of a borrowed prayer-book.   At a sign
They twitched the ensign back and tipped the grating
A creamier bubbling broke the bubbling brine.
The muffled figure tilted to the weighting ;
It dwindled slowly down, slowly gyrating.
Some craned to see ; it dimmed, it disappeared ;
The last green milky bubble blinked and cleared.

" Mister, shake out your reefs," the Captain called.
" Out topsail reefs !" the Mate cried ; then all hands.
Hurried, the great sails shook, and all hands hauled,
Singing that desolate song of lonely lands,
Of how a lover came in dripping bands,
Green with the wet and cold, to tell his lover
That Death was in the sea, and all was over.

Fair came the falling wind ; a seaman said
The Dauber was a Jonah ; once again
The clipper held her course, showing red lead,
Shattering the sea-tops into golden rain.
The waves bowed down before her like blown grain ;
Onwards she thundered, on ; her voyage was short,
Before the tier's bells rang her into port.

DAUBER

Cheerly they rang her in, those beating bells,
The new-come beauty stately from the sea,
Whitening the blue heave of the drowsy swells,
Treading the bubbles down.   With three times three
They cheered her moving beauty in, and she
Came to her berth so noble, so superb ;
Swayed like a queen, and answered to the curb.

Then in the sunset's flush they went aloft,
And unbent sails in that most lovely hour,
When the light gentles and the wind is soft,
And beauty in the heart breaks like a flower.
Working aloft they saw the mountain tower,
Snow to the peak ; they heard the launchmen shout ;
And bright along the bay the lights came out.

And then the night fell dark, and all night long
The pointed mountain pointed at the stars,
Frozen, alert, austere ; the eagle's song
Screamed from her desolate screes and splintered scars.
On her intense crags where the air is sparse
The stars looked down ; their many golden eyes
Watched her and burned, burned out, and came to rise.

DAUBER

Silent the finger of the summit stood,
Icy in pure, thin air, glittering with snows.
Then the sun's coming turned the peak to blood,
And in the rest-house the muleteers arose.
And all day long, where only the eagle goes,
Stones, loosened by the sun, fall; the stones falling
Fill empty gorge on gorge with echoes calling.

EXPLANATIONS OF SOME OF THE SEA TERMS USED IN THE POEM

Backstays. Wire ropes which support the masts against lateral and after strains.

Barney's bull. A figure in marine proverb. A jewel in marine repartee.

Bells. Two bells (one forward, one aft), which are struck every half-hour in a certain manner to mark the passage of the watches.

Bitts. Strong wooden structures (built round each mast) upon which running rigging is secured.

Block. A sheaved pulley.

Boatswain. A supernumerary or idler, generally attached to the mate's watch, and holding considerable authority over the crew.

Bouilli tin. Any tin that contains, or has contained, preserved meat.

Bows. The forward extremity of a ship.

Brace-blocks. Pulleys through which the braces travel.

Braces. Ropes by which the yards are inclined forward or aft.

Bumboat pan. Soft bread sold by the bumboat man, a kind of sea costermonger who trades with ships in port.

Bunt. Those cloths of a square sail which are nearest to the mast when the sail is set. The central portion of a furled square sail. The human abdomen (figuratively).

Buntlines. Ropes which help to confine square sails to the yards in the operation of furling.

Chocks. Wooden stands on which the boats rest.

Cleats. Iron or wooden contrivances to which ropes may be secured.

Clew-lines. Ropes by which the lower corners of square sails are lifted.

Clews. The lower corners of square sails.

Clipper. A title of honour given to ships of more than usual speed and beauty.

Coaming. The raised rim of a hatchway ; a barrier at a doorway to keep water from entering.

Courses. The large square sails set upon the lower yards of sailing ships. The mizen course is called the " crojick."

Cringled. Fitted with iron rings or cringles, many of which are let into sails or sail-roping for various purposes.

Crojick (or cross-jack). A square sail set upon the lower yard of the mizen mast.

Dungarees. Thin blue or khaki-coloured overalls made from cocoanut fibre.

Fairleads. Rings of wood or iron by means of which running rigging is led in any direction.

Fife-rails. Strong wooden shelves fitted with iron pins, to which ropes may be secured.

Fish-hooks. *I.e.*, fingers.

Foot-ropes. Ropes on which men stand when working aloft.

Fo'c'sle. The cabin or cabins in which the men are berthed. It is usually an iron deck-house divided through the middle into two compartments for the two watches, and fitted with wooden bunks. Sometimes it is even fitted with lockers and an iron water-tank.

Foxes. Strands, yarns, or arrangements of yarns of rope.

Freeing-ports. Iron doors in the ship's side which open outwards to free the decks of water.

Frap. To wrap round with rope.

Futtock-shrouds. Iron bars to which the topmast rigging is secured. As they project outward and upward from the masts they are difficult to clamber over.

Galley. The ship's kitchen.

Gantline (girtline). A rope used for the sending of sails up and down from aloft.

Gaskets. Ropes by which the sails are secured in furling.

Half-deck. A cabin or apartment in which the apprentices are berthed. Its situation is usually the ship's waist ; but it is sometimes further aft, and occasionally it is under the poop or even right forward under the top-gallant fo'c'sle.

Halliards. Ropes by which sails are hoisted.

Harness-room. An office or room from which the salt meat is issued, and in which it is sometimes stored.

Hawse. The bows or forward end of a ship.

Head. The forward part of a ship. That upper edge of a square sail which is attached to the yard.

House-flag. The special flag of the firm to which a ship belongs.

Idlers. The members of the round-house mess, generally consisting of the carpenter, cook, sailmaker, boatswain, painter, etc., are known as the idlers.

Jack (or jackstay). An iron bar (fitted along all yards in
sailing ships) to which the head of a square sail is
secured when bent.

Kites. Light upper sails.

Leeches. The outer edges of square sails. In furling some
square sails the leech is dragged inwards till it lies
level with the head upon the surface of the yard.
This is done by the first man who gets upon the yard,
beginning at the weather side.

Logship. A contrivance by which a ship's speed is measured.

Lower topsail. The second sail from the deck on square-
rigged masts. It is a very strong, important sail.

Marline. Tarry line or coarse string made of rope-yarns
twisted together.

Mate. The First or Chief Mate is generally called the
Mate.

Mizen-topmast-head. The summit of the second of the
three or four spars which make the complete mizen-
mast.

Mudhooks. Anchors.

Pins. Iron or wooden bars to which running rigging is
secured.

Pointing. A kind of neat plait with which ropes are sometimes ended off or decorated.

Poop-break. The forward end of the after superstructure.

Ratlines. The rope steps placed across the shrouds to
enable the seamen to go aloft.

Reefers. Apprentices.

Reef-points. Ropes by which the area of some sails may
be reduced in the operation of reefing. Reef-points
are securely fixed to the sails fitted with them, and

when not in use their ends patter continually upon the canvas with a gentle drumming noise.

Reel. A part of the machinery used with a logship.

Round-house. A cabin (of all shapes except round) in which the idlers are berthed.

Royals. Light upper square sails; the fourth, fifth, or sixth sails from the deck according to the mast's rig.

Sail-room. A large room or compartment in which the ship's sails are stored.

"Sails." The sailmaker is meant.

Scuttle-butt. A cask containing fresh water.

Shackles. Rope handles for a sea-chest.

Sheet-blocks. Iron blocks, by means of which sails are sheeted home. In any violent wind they beat upon the mast with great rapidity and force.

Sheets. Ropes or chains which extend the lower corners of square sails in the operation of sheeting home.

Shifting suits (of sails). The operation of removing a ship's sails, and replacing them with others.

Shrouds. Wire ropes of great strength, which support lateral strains on masts.

Shroud-screws. Iron contrivances by which shrouds are hove taut.

Sidelights. A sailing ship carries two of these between sunset and sunrise: one green, to starboard; one red, to port.

Sights. Observations to help in the finding of a ship's position.

Skid. A wooden contrivance on which ship's boats rest.

Skysails. The uppermost square sails; the fifth, sixth, or seventh sails from the deck according to the mast's rig.

DAUBER

Slatting. The noise made by sails flogging in the wind.

Slush. Grease, melted fat.

South-wester. A kind of oilskin hat. A gale from the south-west.

Spit brown. To chew tobacco.

Square sennit. A cunning plait which makes a four-square bar.

Staysails. Fore and aft sails set upon the stays between the masts.

Stow. To furl.

Strop (the, putting on). A strop is a grummet or rope ring. The two players kneel down facing each other, the strop is placed over their heads, and the men then try to pull each other over by the strength of their neck-muscles.

Swing ports. Iron doors in the ship's side which open outwards to free the decks from water.

Tackle (pronounced "taykel"). Blocks, ropes, pulleys, etc.

Take a caulk. To sleep upon the deck.

Topsails. The second and third sails from the deck on the masts of a modern square-rigged ship are known as the lower and upper topsails.

Trucks. The summits of the masts.

Upper topsail. The third square sail from the deck on the masts of square-rigged ships.

Yards. The steel or wooden spars (placed across masts) from which square sails are set.

BILLING AND SONS, LTD., PRINTERS, GUILDFORD